Beautiful Bed Scarves™

General Information

Many of the products used in this pattern book can be purchased from local craft, fabric and variety stores, or from the Annie's Attic Needlecraft Catalog (see Customer Service information on page 16).

Contents

Gilded Age Ripple

SKILL LEVEL

EASY

FINISHED SIZE

Instructions are for full-size bed 23 x 78 inches; changes for queen-size bed 23 x 90 inches and king-size bed 23 x 108 inches are in [ ].

MATERIALS

- NaturallyCaron.com Country medium (worsted) weight yarn (3 oz/185 yds/85g per skein):
  12 [13, 14] skeins #0011 gilded age
- Size G/6/4mm crochet hook or size needed to obtain gauge

4 MEDIUM

GAUGE

4 sc = 1 inch; 3 sc rows and 3 dc rows = 2½ inches

SPECIAL STITCH

Puff stitch (puff st): Yo, insert hook in next st, yo, pull lp through, [yo, insert hook in same st, yo, pull lp through] twice, yo, pull through all 7 lps on hook.

INSTRUCTIONS

SCARF

Row 1 (RS): Ch 105, dc in 5th ch from hook, [**dc dec** *(see Stitch Guide)* in next 2 chs] twice, *ch 1, [**puff st** *(see Special Stitch)* in next ch, ch 1] 5 times, [dc dec in next 2 sts] 6 times, rep from * 4 times, ch 1, [puff st in next ch, ch 1] 5 times, [dc dec in next 2 chs] 3 times, turn. *(36 ch-1 sps, 36 dc, 30 puff sts)*

Row 2: Ch 1, sc in each st and in each ch sp across, turn. *(102 sc)*

Row 3: Ch 2 *(is not used or counted as a st)*, dc in next st, [dc dec in next 2 sts] twice, *ch 1, [puff st in next st, ch 1] 5 times, [dc dec in next 2 sts] 6 times, rep from * 4 times, ch 1, [puff st in next st, ch 1] 5 times, [dc dec in next 2 sts] 3 times, turn. *(36 ch-1 sps, 36 dc, 30 puff sts)*

Rows 4–193 [4–221, 4–265] or to preferred length: [Rep rows 2 and 3 alternately] 95 [109, 131] times.

Row 194 [222, 266]: Rep row 2. Fasten off. ■

Turquoise Treasure

SKILL LEVEL

EASY

FINISHED SIZE

Instructions are for full-size bed 25 x 78 inches; changes for queen-size bed 25 x 92 inches and king-size bed 25 x 108 inches are in [ ].

MATERIALS

4 MEDIUM

- NaturallyCaron.com Country medium (worsted) weight yarn (3 oz/185 yds/85g per skein):
  11 [12, 13] skeins #0005 ocean spray
- Size G/6/4mm crochet hook or size needed to obtain gauge

GAUGE

2 shells and 1 ch sp = 2¼ inches; 6 pattern rows = 3½ inches

PATTERN NOTE

Chain-3 at beginning of row counts as first double crochet unless otherwise stated.

SPECIAL STITCHES

Cluster (cl): Yo, insert hook in indicated st, yo, pull lp through, yo, pull through 2 lps on hook, [yo, insert hook in same st, yo, pull lp through, yo, pull through 2 lps on hook] twice, yo, pull through all 4 lps on hook.

Shell: 5 dc in indicated st or sp.

Picot: Ch 4, sc in 4th ch from hook.

V-stitch (V-st): (2 dc, ch 2, 2 dc) in indicated st or sp.

INSTRUCTIONS

SCARF

Row 1 (RS): Ch 102, sc in 2nd ch from hook and in each ch across, turn. *(101 sc)*

Row 2: **Ch 3** *(see Pattern Note)*, **cl** *(see Special Stitches)* in same st, **picot** *(see Special Stitches)*, sk next 4 sts, *(cl, ch 1, cl) in next st, picot, sk next 4 sts, rep from * across to last st, (cl, dc) in last st, turn. *(40 cls, 20 picots, 19 ch-1 sps, 2 dc)*

Row 3: Ch 3, 2 dc in same st, ch 1, [**shell** *(see Special Stitches)* in next ch-1 sp, ch 1] across, 3 dc in last st, turn. *(19 shells, 6 dc)*

Row 4: Ch 3, (cl, ch 1, cl) in next ch-1 sp, [picot, (cl, ch 1, cl) in next ch sp] across, dc in last st, turn. *(40 cls, 20 ch-1 sps, 19 picots)*

Row 5: Ch 3, shell in next ch-1 sp, [ch 1, shell in next ch-1 sp] across, dc in last st, turn. *(20 shells, 19 ch-1 sps, 2 dc)*

Row 6: Ch 3, cl in same st, picot, *(cl, ch 1, cl) in next ch-1 sp, picot, rep from * across, (cl, dc) in last st, turn. *(40 cls, 20 picots, 19 ch-1 sps)*

Rows 7–126 [7–150, 7–178] or to preferred length: [Rep rows 3–6 consecutively] 30 [36, 43] times.

Row 127 [151, 179]: Ch 1, sc in first st, [ch 4, sc in next ch-1 sp] across, ch 4, sc in last st, turn. *(20 ch sps, 21 sc)*

Row 128 [152, 180]: Ch 1, sc in each st and in each ch across, turn. *(101 sc)*

FIRST END TRIM

Row 1: Ch 3, (dc, ch 2, 2 dc) in same st, [sk next 4 sts, **v-st** *(see Special Stitches)* in next st] across, turn. *(84 dc, 21 ch-2 sps)*

Row 2: Ch 3, dc in next st, ch 2, 2 dc in next ch-2 sp, [dc in sp before next V-st, V-st in ch-2 of next V-st] 19 times, dc in sp before next 2 dc, 2 dc in next ch-2 sp, ch 2, dc in each of last 2 sts, turn. *(104 dc, 21 ch-2 sps)*

Row 3: Ch 3, dc in next st, ch 2, 2 dc in next ch-2 sp, [sk next 2 sts, **fpdc** *(see Stitch Guide)* around next st, V-st in ch-2 sp of next V-st] 19 times, sk next 2 sts, fpdc around next st, 2 dc in next ch-2 sp, ch 2, dc in each of last 2 sts, turn.

Row 4: Ch 3, dc in next st, ch 2, 2 dc in next ch-2 sp, [sk next 2 sts, **bpdc** *(see Stitch Guide)* around next st, (2 dc, ch 2, 2 dc) in next ch-2 sp] 19 times, sk next 2 sts, bpdc around next st, 2 dc in next ch-2 sp, ch 2, dc in each of last 2 sts, turn.

Row 5: Ch 3, dc in next st, 3 dc in next ch-2 sp, [sk next 2 sts, fpdc around next st, 7 dc in next ch-2 sp] 19 times, sk next 2 sts, fpdc around next st, 3 dc in next ch-2 sp, dc in each of last 2 sts. Fasten off.

2ND END TRIM

Row 1: With RS facing, working in starting ch on opposite side of row 1, join with sl st in first ch, ch 3, (dc, ch 2, 2 dc) in same ch, [sk next 4 chs, V-st in next ch] across, turn. *(84 dc, 21 ch-2 sps)*

Rows 2–5: Rep rows 2–5 of First End Trim. ■

Periwinkle **Pizzazz**

SKILL LEVEL

EASY

FINISHED SIZE

Instructions are for full-size bed 22 x 78 inches; changes for queen-size bed 22 x 90 inches and king-size bed 22 x 108 inches are in [ ].

MATERIALS

- NaturallyCaron.com Country medium (worsted) weight yarn (3 oz/185 yds/85g per skein): 9 [10, 11] skeins #0006 berry frappe
- Size K/10½/6.5mm crochet hook or size needed to obtain gauge

4 MEDIUM

GAUGE

3 dc and 1 ch-1 = 1 inch; 4 dc rows and 4 sc rows = 3½ inches

PATTERN NOTE

Chain-3 at beginning of row counts as first double crochet unless otherwise stated.

INSTRUCTIONS

SCARF

Row 1: Ch 91, dc in 4th ch from hook *(first 3 chs count as first dc)* and in each ch across, turn. *(89 dc)*

Row 2: **Ch 3** *(see Pattern Note)*, dc in each of next 3 sts, [ch 1, sk next st, dc in each of next 3 sts] across to last st, dc in last st, turn. *(68 dc, 21 ch sps)*

Row 3: Ch 1, sc in first st, *ch 1, sk next st, **fpsc** *(see Stitch Guide)* around next st, ch 1, sk next st**, sc in next ch sp, rep from * across, ending last rep at **, sc in last st, turn. *(45 sc, 44 ch sps)*

Row 4: Ch 3, *dc in next ch sp, dc in next st, dc in next ch sp**, ch 1, sk next st, rep from * across, ending last rep at **, dc in last st, turn. *(68 dc, 21 ch sps)*

Rows 5–178 [5–206, 5–246] or to preferred length: [Rep rows 3 and 4 alternately] 87 [101, 121] times.

Row 179 [207, 247]: Ch 3, dc in each st across. Fasten off.

FRINGE

For each Fringe, cut 3 strands, each 18 inches long. With 3 strands help tog, fold in half, insert hook in st, pull fold through st, pull all loose ends through fold, and tighten. Trim

Attach 1 Fringe to every other st on each short end of Scarf. ■

Terra-Cotta

SKILL LEVEL

INTERMEDIATE

FINISHED SIZE

Instructions are for full-size bed $23\frac{1}{2}$ x $77\frac{1}{2}$ inches; changes for queen-size bed $23\frac{1}{2}$ x $89\frac{1}{2}$ inches and king-size bed $23\frac{1}{2}$ x $109\frac{1}{2}$ inches are in [ ].

MATERIALS

- Lion Brand Cotton-Ease medium (worsted) weight yarn ($3\frac{1}{2}$ oz/207 yds/100g per ball):
  11 [12, 13] balls #134 terra-cotta
- Sizes H/8/5mm and J/10/6mm crochet hooks or size needed to obtain gauge

4 MEDIUM

GAUGE

Size J hook: 14 sc = 4 inches

PATTERN NOTE

Chain-3 at beginning of row or round counts as first double crochet unless otherwise stated.

SPECIAL STITCH

Block stitch (block st): [Yo, insert hook around post of last dc made, yo, pull up lp] 4 times, yo, pull through all lps on hook, ch 1.

INSTRUCTIONS

SCARF

Row 1: With size J hook, ch 266 [308, 378], sc in 2nd ch from hook and in each ch across, turn. *(265 [307, 377] sc)*

Rows 2–4: Ch 1, sc in each st across, turn.

Row 5: With size H hook, **ch 3** *(see Pattern Note)*, dc in next st, **block st** *(see Special Stitch)*, [sk next st, dc in next st, block st] across to last st, dc in last st, turn.

Row 6: Ch 1, sc in sp between first 2 sts, [2 sc in sp between next 2 block sts] across, sc in 3rd ch of beg ch-3, turn.

Rows 7–10: With size J hook, ch 1, sc in each st across, turn.

Next rows: Rep rows 5–10 consecutively for pattern until piece measures 23 inches or desired width, ending with row 9. **Do not turn or fasten off** at end of last row.

BORDER

Row 1: Working in ends of rows, evenly sp sc across. Fasten off.

Row 2: With size J hook, join with sc in end of first row on opposite side, evenly sp sc across ends of rows. Fasten off.

Rnd 3: Now working in rnds around entire outer edge, with size H hook, join with sl st in first st of last row on Scarf, ch 3, 4 dc in same st, sk next 2 sts, sc in next st, sk next 2 sts, [5 dc in next st, sk next 2 sts, sc in next st, sk next 2 sts] around, sk more or less sts on last rep as needed, join with sl st in 3rd ch of beg ch-3. Fasten off. ■

Irish Moss

SKILL LEVEL

INTERMEDIATE

FINISHED SIZE

Instructions are for full-size bed 24 x 78 inches; changes for queen-size bed 24 x 90 inches and king-size bed 24 x 108 inches are in [ ].

MATERIALS

- Premier Yarns Harmony chunky (bulky) weight yarn (3½ oz/ 120 yds/100g per skein):
  - 9 [10, 11] skeins #34-110 asparagus
  - 4 [5, 6] skeins #34-111 thyme
- Sizes G/6/4mm and H/8/5mm crochet hooks or size needed to obtain gauge

5 BULKY

GAUGE

Size H hook: 2 extended shells = 3 inches; 5 extended shell rows = 3 inches

PATTERN NOTES

Chain-3 at beginning of row counts as first double crochet unless otherwise stated.

Join with slip stitch as indicated unless otherwise stated.

SPECIAL STITCHES

Shell: (2 dc, ch 2, 2 dc) in indicated place.

Extended shell (ext shell): Yo, insert hook in ch-2 sp of next shell on row before last, yo, pull up long lp, complete as dc, shell in next shell on last row, yo, insert hook in same ch sp as first dc, yo, pull up long lp, complete as dc.

INSTRUCTIONS

SCARF

Row 1: With size H hook and asparagus, ch 55, **shell** *(see Special Stitches)* in 5th ch from hook *(first 3 chs count as first dc)*, [sk next 3 chs, shell in next ch] across to last 2 chs, sk next ch, dc in last ch, turn. *(13 shells, 2 dc)*

Row 2: Ch 3 *(see Pattern Notes)*, [yo, insert hook in same ch as next shell was worked, yo, pull up long lp, complete as dc, shell in ch sp of next shell, yo, insert hook in same ch as first dc was worked, yo, pull up long lp, complete as dc] across to last st, dc in last st, turn.

Rows 3–123 [3–143, 3–173] or to preferred length less 4 inches: Ch 3, **ext shell** *(see Special Stitches)* across to last st, dc in last st, turn.

Last row: Ch 1, sk ch sps, sc in each st across. Fasten off.

BORDER

Rnd 1: Working in sts and ends of rows, evenly sp sts so piece lies flat, with size G hook and thyme, join with sc in any st, sc around with 3 sc in each corner, **join** *(see Pattern Notes)* in beg sc.

Rnd 2: Ch 1, sc in first st, tr in next st, [sc in next st, tr in next st] around with (sc, tr, sc) in each center corner st, join in beg sc.

Rnd 3: Ch 1, sc in each st around with 3 sc in each center corner st, join in beg sc.

Rnds 4–7: [Rep rnds 2 and 3 alternately] twice. Fasten off at end of last rnd. ■

Linen & Lace

SKILL LEVEL

INTERMEDIATE

FINISHED SIZE

Instructions are for full-size bed 25 x 79 inches; changes for queen-size bed 25 x 91 inches and king-size bed 25 x 109 inches are in [ ].

MATERIALS

- Aunt Lydia's Fashion Crochet size 3 crochet cotton (150 yds per ball):
  10 [12, 13] balls #226 natural
- Aunt Lydia's Classic Crochet size 10 crochet cotton (350 yds per ball):
  1 ball each #226 natural and #475 dusty rose
- Sizes 1/2.25mm and 9/1.25mm steel crochet hooks or size needed to obtain gauge
- Tapestry needle
- Sewing needle
- 5-inch linen squares: 52 [60, 72]
- Natural sewing thread

GAUGE

Size 1 hook: Motif = 6-inches square

PATTERN NOTES

Join with slip stitch as indicted unless otherwise stated.

For each linen square, turn edges under 1/4 inch, then turn under 1/4 inch again, sew to secure.

SPECIAL STITCHES

Beginning cluster (beg cl): Ch 3, yo twice, insert hook in indicated place, yo, pull lp through, [yo, pull through 2 lps on hook] twice, yo twice, insert hook in same place, yo, pull lp through, [yo, pull through 2 lps on hook] twice, yo, pull through all 3 lps on hook.

Cluster (cl): Yo twice, insert hook in indicated place, yo, pull lp through, [yo, pull through 2 lps on hook] twice, *yo twice, insert hook in same place, yo, pull lp through, [yo, pull through 2 lps on hook] twice, rep from *, yo, pull through all 4 lps on hook.

Picot: Ch 3, sl st in top of last st made.

INSTRUCTIONS

FIRST ROW

FIRST MOTIF

Rnd 1: With size 1 hook and size 3 crochet cotton, insert hook through corner of 1 linen square, yo, pull lp through, complete as sc, 2 sc in same place, evenly sp 20 sc across each side of square with 3 sc in each corner, **join** *(see Pattern Notes)* in beg sc. *(92 sc)*

Rnd 2: Ch 1, sc in first st, *[ch 5, sc in next st] twice, [ch 5, sk next 2 sts, sc in next st] 6 times, ch 5, sk next 2 sts**, sc in next st, rep from * around, ending last rep at **, join in beg sc. *(36 ch sps)*

Rnd 3: [Sl st, **beg cl** *(see Special Stitches)*, ch 3, **cl** *(see Special Stitches)*] in first ch sp, *ch 3, (cl, ch 3, cl) in next ch sp, [ch 3, sc in next ch sp, ch 3, (cl, ch 3, cl) in next ch sp] 3 times, ch 3, sc in next ch sp, ch 3**, (cl, ch 3, cl) in next ch sp, rep from * around, ending last rep at **, join in top of beg cl. Fasten off.

2ND MOTIF

Rnds 1 & 2: Rep rnds 1 and 2 of First Motif.

Rnd 3: (Sl st, beg cl, ch 3, cl) in first ch sp, ch 3, joining to side of last Motif, (cl, ch 1, sl st in corresponding ch-3 sp on other Motif, ch 1, cl) in next ch-5 sp, [ch 3, sc in next ch sp, ch 3, (cl, ch 1, sl st in next ch-3 sp on other Motif, ch 1, cl) in next ch sp] 4 times, *ch 3, (cl, ch 3, cl) in next ch sp, [ch 3, sc in next ch sp, ch 3, (cl, ch 3, cl) in next ch sp] 4 times, rep from *, ch 3, (cl, ch 3, cl) in next ch sp, [ch 3, sc in next ch sp, ch 3, (cl, ch 3, cl) in next ch sp] 3 times, ch 3, sc in next ch sp, ch 3, join in top of beg cl. Fasten off.

Rep 2nd Motif twice for a total of 4 Motifs on this row.

2ND ROW

FIRST MOTIF

Joining to the bottom of the First Motif on last row, work First Row 2nd Motif.

2ND MOTIF

Rnds 1 & 2: Rep rnds 1 and 2 of First Row First Motif.

Rnd 3: (Sl st, beg cl, ch 3, cl) in first ch sp, ch 3, joining to bottom of next Motif on row above, *(cl, ch 1, sl st in corresponding ch-3 sp on other Motif, ch 1, cl) in next ch-5 sp, [ch 3, sc in next ch sp, ch 3, (cl, ch 1, sl st in next ch-3 sp on other Motif, ch 1, cl) in next ch sp] 4 times*, working on side of last Motif on this row, ch 3, rep between * once, ch 3, (cl, ch 3, cl) in next ch sp, [ch 3, sc in next ch sp, ch 3, (cl, ch 3, cl) in next ch sp] 4 times, ch 3, (cl, ch 3, cl) in next ch sp, [ch 3, sc in next ch sp, ch 3, (cl, ch 3, cl) in next ch sp] 3 times, ch 3, sc in next ch sp, ch 3, join in top of beg cl. Fasten off.

Rep 2nd Motif twice for a total of 4 Motifs on this row.

Rep 2nd row 11 [13, 16] times for a total of 13 [15, 18] rows.

EDGING

With size 1 hook and size 3 crochet cotton, join in corner ch-3 sp before 1 short end, beg cl in same sp, **picot** *(see Special Stitches)*, **ch 5, sc in top of next cl, *ch 5, cl in next ch sp, picot, [ch 5, sc in next ch sp, ch 2, sc in next ch sp, ch 5, cl in next ch-3 sp, picot] 4 times, ch 5, sc in next ch sp, ch 2, sc in next corner ch sp on next Motif, rep from * across to next corner Motif, ch 5, cl in next ch sp, picot, [ch 5, sc in next ch sp, ch 2, sc in next ch sp, ch 5, cl in next ch-3 sp, picot] 4 times, ch 5, sc in top of next cl, ch 5***, cl in next center corner ch sp, picot, rep from ** around, ending last rep at ***, join in top of beg cl. Fasten off.

FLOWER

MAKE 36 [42, 51].

With size 9 hook and natural size 10 crochet cotton, ch 4, 11 dc in 4th ch from hook *(first 3 chs count as first dc)*, join in 3rd ch of beg ch-3. Fasten off. *(12 dc)*

PETALS

With size 9 hook, join dusty rose with sl st in any st, *ch 9, sc in 2nd ch from hook, hdc in next ch, dc in each of next 2 chs, tr in each of next 3 chs, dc in last ch, sk next st on last rnd**, sl st in next st, rep from * around, ending last rep at **, join in beg sl st. Fasten off. *(6 Petals).*

Tack 1 Flower to each sp between joined Motifs. ■

Stitch Guide

For more complete information, visit **FreePatterns.com**

ABBREVIATIONS

beg	begin/begins/beginning
bpdc	back post double crochet
bpsc	back post single crochet
bptr	back post treble crochet
CC	contrasting color
ch(s)	chain(s)
ch-	refers to chain or space previously made (e.g., ch-1 space)
ch sp(s)	chain space(s)
cl(s)	cluster(s)
cm	centimeter(s)
dc	double crochet (singular/plural)
dc dec	double crochet 2 or more stitches together, as indicated
dec	decrease/decreases/decreasing
dtr	double treble crochet
ext	extended
fpdc	front post double crochet
fpsc	front post single crochet
fptr	front post treble crochet
g	gram(s)
hdc	half double crochet
hdc dec	half double crochet 2 or more stitches together, as indicated
inc	increase/increases/increasing
lp(s)	loop(s)
MC	main color
mm	millimeter(s)
oz	ounce(s)
pc	popcorn(s)
rem	remain/remains/remaining
rep(s)	repeat(s)
rnd(s)	round(s)
RS	right side
sc	single crochet (singular/plural)
sc dec	single crochet 2 or more stitches together, as indicated
sk	skip/skipped/skipping
sl st(s)	slip stitch(es)
sp(s)	space/spaces/spaced
st(s)	stitch(es)
tog	together
tr	treble crochet
trtr	triple treble
WS	wrong side
yd(s)	yard(s)
yo	yarn over

Chain—ch: Yo, pull through lp on hook.

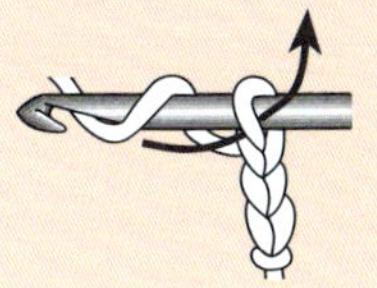

Slip stitch—sl st: Insert hook in st, pull through both lps on hook.

Single crochet—sc: Insert hook in st, yo, pull through st, yo, pull through both lps on hook.

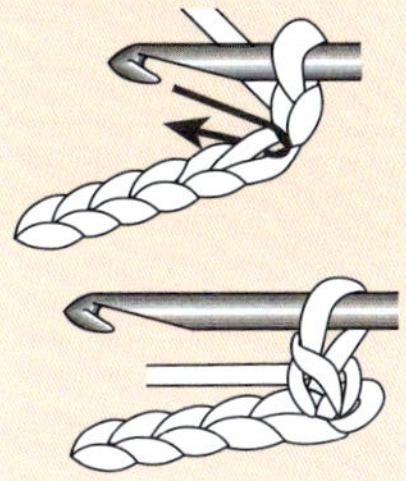

Front post stitch—fp:
Back post stitch—bp: When working post st, insert hook from right to left around post st on previous row.

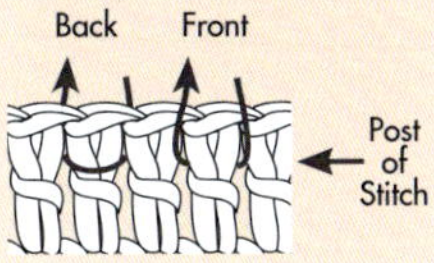

Front loop—front lp
Back loop—back lp

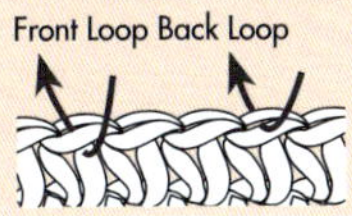

Half double crochet—hdc: Yo, insert hook in st, yo, pull through st, yo, pull through all 3 lps on hook.

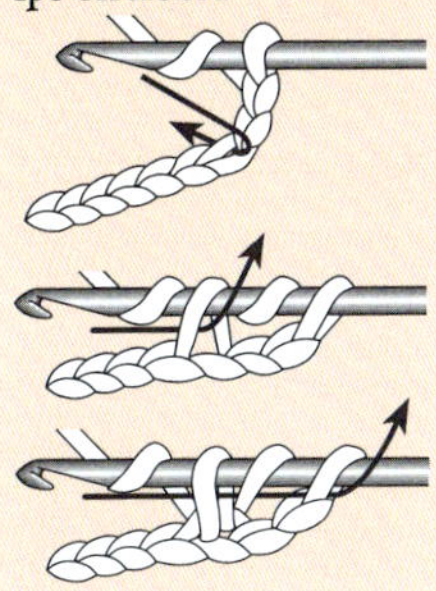

Double crochet—dc: Yo, insert hook in st, yo, pull through st, [yo, pull through 2 lps] twice.

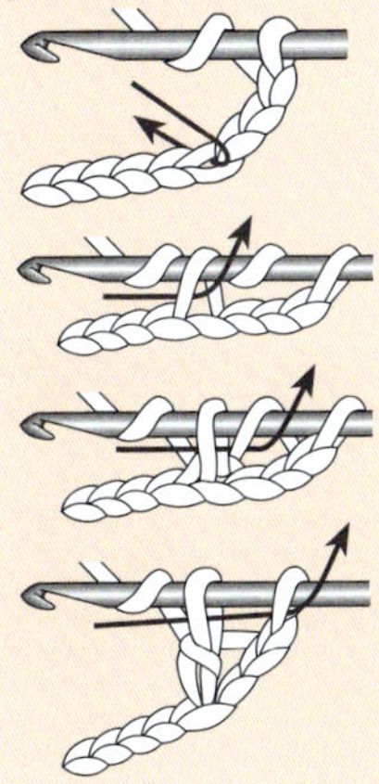

Change colors: Drop first color; with 2nd color, pull through last 2 lps of st.

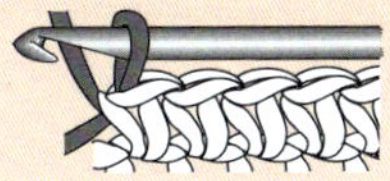

Treble crochet—tr: Yo twice, insert hook in st, yo, pull through st, [yo, pull through 2 lps] 3 times.

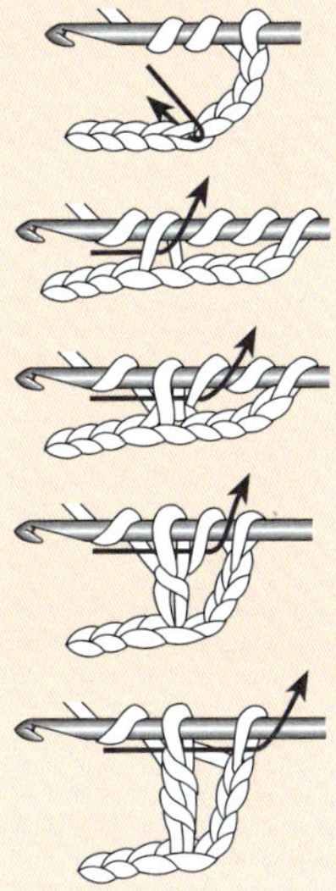

Double treble crochet—dtr: Yo 3 times, insert hook in st, yo, pull through st, [yo, pull through 2 lps] 4 times.

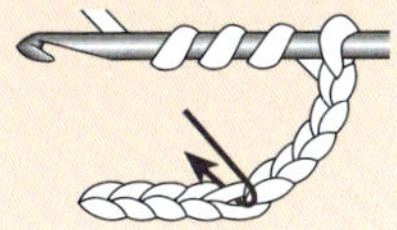

Single crochet decrease (sc dec): (Insert hook, yo, draw lp through) in each of the sts indicated, yo, draw through all lps on hook.

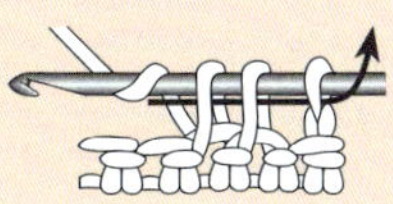

Example of 2-sc dec

Half double crochet decrease (hdc dec): (Yo, insert hook, yo, draw lp through) in each of the sts indicated, yo, draw through all lps on hook.

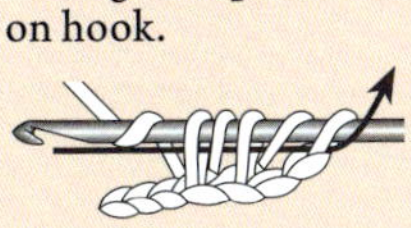

Example of 2-hdc dec

Double crochet decrease (dc dec): (Yo, insert hook, yo, draw loop through, draw through 2 lps on hook) in each of the sts indicated, yo, draw through all lps on hook.

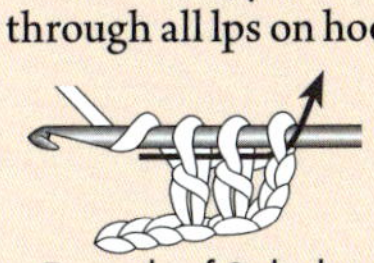

Example of 2-dc dec

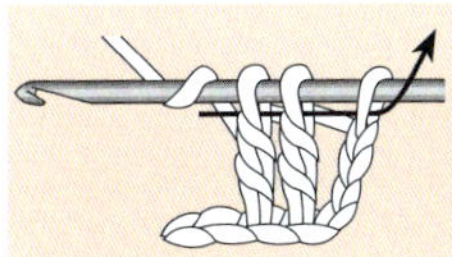

Example of 2-tr dec

Treble crochet decrease (tr dec): Holding back last lp of each st, tr in each of the sts indicated, yo, pull through all lps on hook.

US		**UK**
sl st (slip stitch)	=	sc (single crochet)
sc (single crochet)	=	dc (double crochet)
hdc (half double crochet)	=	htr (half treble crochet)
dc (double crochet)	=	tr (treble crochet)
tr (treble crochet)	=	dtr (double treble crochet)
dtr (double treble crochet)	=	ttr (triple treble crochet)
skip	=	miss

Metric Conversion Charts

METRIC CONVERSIONS				
yards	x	.9144	=	metres (m)
yards	x	91.44	=	centimetres (cm)
inches	x	2.54	=	centimetres (cm)
inches	x	25.40	=	millimetres (mm)
inches	x	.0254	=	metres (m)

centimetres	x	.3937	=	inches
metres	x	1.0936	=	yards

INCHES INTO MILLIMETRES & CENTIMETRES (Rounded off slightly)

inches	mm	cm	inches	cm	inches	cm	inches	cm
1/8	3	0.3	5	12.5	21	53.5	38	96.5
1/4	6	0.6	5 1/2	14	22	56	39	99
3/8	10	1	6	15	23	58.5	40	101.5
1/2	13	1.3	7	18	24	61	41	104
5/8	15	1.5	8	20.5	25	63.5	42	106.5
3/4	20	2	9	23	26	66	43	109
7/8	22	2.2	10	25.5	27	68.5	44	112
1	25	2.5	11	28	28	71	45	114.5
1 1/4	32	3.2	12	30.5	29	73.5	46	117
1 1/2	38	3.8	13	33	30	76	47	119.5
1 3/4	45	4.5	14	35.5	31	79	48	122
2	50	5	15	38	32	81.5	49	124.5
2 1/2	65	6.5	16	40.5	33	84	50	127
3	75	7.5	17	43	34	86.5		
3 1/2	90	9	18	46	35	89		
4	100	10	19	48.5	36	91.5		
4 1/2	115	11.5	20	51	37	94		

KNITTING NEEDLES CONVERSION CHART

Canada/U.S.	0	1	2	3	4	5	6	7	8	9	10	10½	11	13	15
Metric (mm)	2	2¼	2¾	3¼	3½	3¾	4	4½	5	5½	6	6½	8	9	10

CROCHET HOOKS CONVERSION CHART

Canada/U.S.	1/B	2/C	3/D	4/E	5/F	6/G	8/H	9/I	10/J	10½/K	N
Metric (mm)	2.25	2.75	3.25	3.5	3.75	4.25	5	5.5	6	6.5	9.0

Annie's Attic®

TOLL-FREE ORDER LINE or to request a free catalog (800) LV-ANNIE (800) 582-6643
Customer Service (800) AT-ANNIE (800) 282-6643, **Fax** (800) 882-6643
Visit AnniesAttic.com

ISBN: 978-1-59635-300-8

Printed in USA

1 2 3 4 5 6 7 8 9